THE TERRY DIARY

The Field Diary of

GENERAL ALFRED H. TERRY

The Yellowstone Expedition -1876

COPYRIGHT 2014 BIG BYTE BOOKS

Get more great reading from BIG BYTE BOOKS

Contents
PUBLISHER'S NOTES..1
THE OFFICIAL REPORT 4
THE FIELD DIARY..18

PUBLISHER'S NOTES

THE Battle of the Little Bighorn and the commander of the 7th Cavalry, General George Armstrong Custer, remain as controversial and likely to be divisive in any conversation of history as much today as they did 139 years ago. Why is this so?

Whatever your opinion of General Custer, military assessments of his actions at the Little Bighorn find little fault outside of the fact that he had insufficient intelligence and erroneous expectations of warrior behavior. Custer was an experienced and well-regarded cavalry leader dating from his service in the American Civil War. A very good account of his time in the Civil War is James Kidd's memoir of his time with *Custer's Michigan Brigade*.

Fighting Indians was a different kind of warfare than the set-piece battles of the Civil War. As with all asymmetrical warfare, Native Americans mostly employed guerilla-style tactics. Their main concern when attacked in a village was to protect women and children and get them away. They had no interest in fighting against cannons and Gatling guns, which they had neither expertise in or supplies.

Unlike other Indian fights that most of the army men at the Little Bighorn had experienced, the Indians were present in vastly larger numbers and instead of dispersing, which was Custer's greatest concern, the Indians stood and fought fiercely.

George Custer was an ambitious man who was reaching an age where commanding troops in the field was probably not going to fulfill the vision that he and his wife, Libby, had for his life. According to some of his Native American scouts on the Yellowstone Expedition, he told them this was his last campaign and that once he became the Great Father in Washington, he would take care of their tribes (see *Custer's Scouts at the Little Bighorn*). Custer was interested in and apparently pretty good with Indian sign language. Although he used interpreters for issuing orders, he could converse with his scouts in sign.

As you'll read below in the diary of General Alfred Terry, both Major Marcus Reno and Lieutenant-Colonel Custer got under Terry's skin for what he felt were disobedience of orders. He apparently did not feel these infractions were serious enough to remove either from command.

No less person that President Ulysses S. Grant did not want Custer on the expedition. He was irritated with Custer for having given testimony to Congress, which was little more than hearsay, about corruption in awards of contracts to supply forts—testimony that not only implicated Grant's Secretary of War, William Belknap, but Grant's brother Orvil as well. Generals Terry and Philip Sheridan interceded on Custer's behalf and Grant acquiesced to Custer's taking command of his regiment. Terry would command the expedition and Custer was ordered not to take any reporters with him. He was accompanied by reporter Marc Kellogg, who died near Custer Hill.

When Custer and five companies of the 7th Cavalry were wiped out, the United States was just days away from its Centennial celebration. The battle resulted in the demise of a famous, flamboyant, and popular Civil War hero. White Americans, with an unshakeable belief in Manifest Destiny and their own superiority, could not believe a band of "savages" could defeat the best cavalry regiment in the country. The deaths on June 25th, 1876 represented a full one percent of the entire U.S. Army. The event left the country in shock and disbelief.

The 7th Cavalry survivors, despite whatever trauma the men experienced over the two days of battle, continued to hunt for the Sioux for the rest of the summer. They did not find them. They returned to Fort Abraham Lincoln in September.

In 1879, an army inquiry was convened in Chicago at the request of Major Marcus Reno. He had been accused of cowardice and blamed for the deaths at the Little Bighorn. The transcript of the _Reno Court of Inquiry_ is one of the most important documents in U.S. military history and is fascinating to read. The original transcript was almost lost to history because it has been accessed by researchers so many times.

One other diary from the Yellowstone Expedition deserves mention here. Lieutenant Edward Settle Godfrey (later General) was commanding K Company under Captain Frederick Benteen on the expedition. His diary is full of interesting observations of various characters in this drama, including Custer. For more, see _The Godfrey Diary_.

THE OFFICIAL REPORT

OF GENERAL A. H. TERRY

The report of Gen. Terry is found in House of Representatives Executive Document I, Part 2, 44th Congress, 2nd Session, Report of the Secretary of War. Volume I, Washington, D.C. 1876. The portion appended here refers only to the Yellowstone Expedition.

On the 19th of February I was informed, by a dispatch of that date from Maj. James S. Brisbin, Second Cavalry, commanding the post of Fort Ellis, that he had on the previous day received an appeal for help from a party who had established themselves for the purpose of trade, trapping, and mining at a point near the mouth of the Big Horn, known as Fort Pease. It was stated that fourteen men were holding a stockade against the Indians, who had surrounded them. Major Brisbin proposed to go to their relief. The proposal of Major Brisbin was approved by me, and he was instructed by telegraph to proceed at once to carry it into effect. He marched from Fort Ellis on the 21st of February with four companies of his regiment and arrived at Fort Pease and relieved the occupants on the 4th of March. It was found that the original party had consisted of forty-six men, of whom six had been killed, and eight wounded, thirteen had escaped by night, and nineteen were found in the stockade and were brought away. No Indians were seen by the troops, but war-lodges were found representing a force of about sixty Sioux who had fled southward.

On the 10th of February last I received from the Lieutenant-General commanding orders to commence operations against the hostile Sioux. At the same time I was informed that similar instructions had been given to Brigadier-General Crook, then as now commanding the Department of the Platte, who would operate from Fort Laramie in the direction of the head-waters of Powder River, Pumpkin Butte, and the Big Horn. Preparations for the movement were immediately commenced, and it was supposed that the troops could be made ready to march early in April. The collection of troops and supplies for the expedition, however, was dependent on the opening of the Northern Pacific Railroad.

That road was opened earlier than is usual in the spring, but severe snow-storms again closed it. Owing to this fact, and to the necessity of waiting for the arrival of troops ordered from the Department of the Gulf to this Department, it was not until the middle of May that all preparations were completed.

The force originally intended for the field consisted of the nine companies of the Seventh Cavalry then in this Department. Companies C and G of the Seventeenth Infantry, Company B of the Sixth Infantry, a battery of Gatling guns, manned by detachments from the Twentieth Infantry, and forty Indian scouts. Subsequently it was increased by the three remaining companies of the Seventh Cavalry, which, on my application, were ordered from the Department of the Gulf to their regiment, in order that they might accompany it into the field.

Lieut.-Col. G. A. Custer, of the Seventh Cavalry, was at first assigned to the command of this force; but under subsequent instructions I assumed the command in person, Lieutenant-Colonel Custer being assigned to the command of his regiment.

On the 27th of February I directed Col. John Gibbon, of the Seventh Infantry, commanding the district of Montana, to prepare for the field all the troops which could be spared from the garrisons in his district, and to be ready to march from Fort Ellis down the valley of the Yellowstone. These orders were crossed on their way to Montana by a dispatch from Colonel Gibbon, in which he suggested the same movement.

On the 25th of February a telegram was sent to Colonel Gibbon in which he was directed not only to make his preparations, but to move as soon as he should be able. The force available for the movement consisted of four companies of the Second Cavalry and six companies of the Seventh Infantry. It was collected as rapidly as possible, and it started from Fort Ellis on the 3d of April. For the details of Colonel Gibbon's march until he made a junction with the column under my own command, I refer to his report, which is forwarded herewith. It was not intended that this column should seek for and attack the hostile Sioux independently, unless, indeed, some favorable opportunity should present itself. Its duty was to guard the left bank of the Yellowstone, and, if possible, prevent the Indians from crossing it in case that they should attempt to do so, either in pursuance of their habit of following the herds of buffalo to the north during the summer, or in case they should seek to avoid the troops coming from the south and the east.

This duty was admirably performed. Colonel Gibbon advanced to the mouth of the Rosebud, and from that point kept detachments moving up and down the Yellowstone.

It is of course impossible to say whether the Indians would or would not have crossed the latter stream had not Colonel Gibbon's force occupied its left bank, but my own opinion is that they would have done so.

To supply the forces in the field, subsistence and forage were sent up the Yellowstone, by steamer, to Stanley's stockade, near the mouth of Glendive Creek. With them was sent a guard of three companies of the Sixth Infantry, under command of Major o. H. Moore, of that regiment. The departure of the boats from Fort Lincoln was so timed as to bring them to their destination a short time in advance of the presumed arrival of the troops at the same point.

No train of pack-mules has ever been organized in this department, and the marching columns were necessarily dependent on wagons for the transport of their supplies. There were, however, carried in wagons about 250 pack-saddles to be placed on the mules of the train in an emergency.

I arrived personally at Fort Lincoln on the 10th of May. Soon after my arrival I received information from more than one independent source which led me to believe that the main body of the hostile Sioux was on the Little Missouri River, and between that stream and the Yellowstone. I therefore sent to Fort Ellis a telegraphic dispatch, to be forwarded to Colonel Gibbon, directing him to move down the Yellowstone to "Stanley's stockade," to cross the river, and move out on "Stanley's trail" to meet the column from Lincoln. This column marched on the morning of May 17. For some days its progress was slow, for the wagons were heavily laden and recent rains had made the ground extremely soft.

The Little Missouri was reached on May 29. Here a halt was made for a day in order that the valley of the river might be reconnoitered. This was done by Lieutenant-Colonel Custer with a portion of his regiment, but no indications of the recent presence of Indians were discovered. The march was resumed on the 31st; but on the 1st and 2d of June a heavy snow-storm detained the column on the edge of the bad lands which border the left banks of the Little Missouri. On the 3d Beaver Creek was reached. In the morning of that day scouts, sent out by Major Moore from the Yellowstone, brought me dispatches from that officer and from Colonel Gibbon also. From the scouts I learned that there were no traces of Indians between "Stanley's stockade" and Beaver Creek; by the dispatches I was informed that the steamers with supplies had reached their destination, and that Colonel Gibbon, having received the dispatch sent to him from Fort Lincoln, was marching down the Yellowstone. Upon this information I determined to move Up Beaver Creek, and thence march directly to Powder River. Orders were therefore sent to Colonel Gibbon to suspend his movements and to Major Moore to send one boat-load of supplies to the mouth of the Powder.

On the morning of the 4th the march was again resumed, our course being up the Beaver. On the 6th we turned again to the west, and in the evening of the 7th reached Powder River at a point about twenty miles from the Yellowstone.

On the 8th, leaving the column in camp, I went with an escort to the mouth of the Powder, and there found the steamer *Far West* with supplies.

The next day I went on the steamer up the Yellowstone to meet Colonel Gibbon. I met him at a point ten or fifteen miles below the mouth of the Tongue, and gave him instructions to return with his troops to the mouth of the Rosebud. Returning, I gave orders for the transfer of all troops and supplies from the stockade to a depot to be established at the mouth of the Powder, and thence proceeded to the camp of the column.

The next day Maj. M. A. Reno, Seventh Cavalry, with six companies of his regiment and one Gatling gun, was directed to reconnoiter the valley of the Powder as far as the forks of the river, then to cross to Mizpah Creek, to descend that creek to near its mouth, thence to cross to Tongue River and descend to its mouth. He was provided with rations for ten days, carried on pack-saddles. On the 11th the remainder of the column marched to the Yellowstone, where it remained until the 15th, in order to give time for Major Reno's movements. During this interval the troops at the stockade, and all the supplies which had been landed there, were brought up. On the morning of the 15th, Lieutenant-Colonel Custer, with six companies of his regiment, one Gatling gun, and a train of pack-mules, marched for Tongue River, all the wagons with their infantry-guard having been left at the depot. He reached the Tongue on the 16th. Here we waited for news from Major Reno until the evening of the 19th, when a dispatch was received from him, by which it appeared that he had crossed to the Rosebud and found a heavy Indian trail; and that after following it for some distance he had retraced his steps, had descended the stream to its mouth, and was then on his way to the Tongue. Orders were at once sent to him to halt and await the arrival of Lieutenant-Colonel Custer; and the latter was instructed to march the next morning for the mouth of the Rosebud. He arrived at this last-named point on the 21st. On the same day Colonel Gibbon's column was put in motion for a point on the north bank of the Yellowstone, opposite the mouth of the Big Horn; with it were sent the Gatling guns which had until this time accompanied the Seventh Cavalry.

At a conference which took place on the 21st between Colonel Gibbon, Lieutenant-Colonel Custer, and myself, I communicated to them the plan of operations which I had decided to adopt. It was that Colonel Gibbon's column should cross the Yellowstone near the mouth of the Little Big Horn, and thence up that stream, with the expectation that it would arrive at the last-named point by the 26th; that Lieutenant-Colonel Custer with the whole of the Seventh Cavalry should proceed up the Rosebud until he should ascertain the direction in which the trail discovered by Major Reno led; that if it led to the Little Big Horn it should not be followed; but that

Lieutenant-Colonel Custer should keep still farther to the south before turning toward that river, in order to intercept the Indians should they attempt to pass around his left, and in order, by a longer march, to give time for Colonel Gibbon's column to come up.

This plan was founded on the belief that at some point on the Little Big Horn a body of hostile Sioux would be found; and that although it was impossible to make movements in perfect concert, as might have been done had there been a known fixed objective point to be reached, yet, by the judicious use of the excellent guides and scouts which we possessed, the two columns might be brought within co-operating distance of each other, so that either of them which should be first engaged might be a "waiting fight" give time for the other to come up. At the same time it was thought that a double attack would very much diminish the chances of a successful retreat by the Sioux, should they be disinclined to fight. It was believed to be impracticable to join Colonel Gibbon's column to Lieutenant-Colonel Custer's force; for more than one-half of Colonel Gibbon's troops were infantry, who would be unable to keep up with cavalry in a rapid movement; while to detach Gibbon's mounted men and add them to the Seventh Cavalry would leave his force too small to act as an independent body.

The written instructions given to Lieutenant-Colonel Custer were as follows:

Headquarters Department of Dakota, (In the Field,)

Camp at Mouth of Rosebud River, Montana, June 22, 1876.

Colonel: The brigadier-general commanding directs that as soon as your regiment can be made ready for the march, you proceed up the Rosebud in pursuit of the Indians whose trail was discovered by Major Reno a few days since. It is, of course, impossible to give you any definite instructions in regard to this movement; and were it not impossible to do so, the department commander places too much confidence in your zeal, energy, and ability to wish to impose upon you precise orders, which might hamper your action when nearly in contact with the enemy. He will, however, indicate to you his own views of what your action should be, and he desires that you should conform to them unless you shall see sufficient reason for departing from them. He thinks that you should proceed up the Rosebud until you ascertain definitely the direction in which the trail above spoken of leads. Should it be found (as it appears to be almost certain that it will be found) to turn toward the Little Horn, he thinks that you should still proceed southward, perhaps as far as the headwaters of the Tongue, and then turn toward the Little Horn, feeling constantly, however, to your left, so as to preclude the possibility of the escape of the Indians to the south or southeast by passing around your left flank.

The column of Colonel Gibbon is now in motion for the mouth of the Big Horn. As soon as it reaches that point it will cross the Yellowstone and move up at least as far as the forks of the Little and Big Horns. Of course its future movements must be controlled by circumstances as they arise; but it is hoped that the Indians if upon the Little Horn, may be so nearly inclosed by the two columns that their escape will be impossible. The department commander desires that on your way up the Rosebud you should thoroughly examine the upper part of Tullock's Creek; and that you should endeavor to send a scout through to Colonel Gibbon's column with information of the result of your examination. The lower part of this creek will be examined by a detachment from Colonel Gibbon's command.

The supply-steamer will be pushed up the Big Horn as far as the forks, if the river is found to be navigable for that distance; and the department commander (who will accompany the column of Colonel Gibbon) desires you to report to him there not later than the expiration of the time for which your troops are rationed, unless in the mean time you receive further orders.

Very respectfully, your obedient servant,

ED. W. SMITH.
Captain, Eighteenth Infantry, A.A.A.G.

Lieut. Col. G. A. Custer,
Seventh Cavalry.

The movements which followed have already been reported in telegraphic dispatches sent to the headquarters of the division from the field. These dispatches, however, were very imperfectly transmitted. I therefore repeat them here:

[Telegram]
Headquarters Department of Dakota,
Camp on Little Big Horn River, Montana, June 27, 1876.
To the Adjutant-General of the Military Division of the Missouri, Chicago, Ill., via Fort Ellis:

It is my painful duty to report that day before yesterday, the 25th instant, a great disaster overtook General Custer and the troops under his command. At 12 o'clock of the 22d, he started with his whole regiment and a strong detachment of scouts and guides from the mouth of the Rosebud. Proceeding up that river about twenty miles, he struck a very heavy Indian trail which had previously been discovered, and, pursuing it, found that it led, as it was supposed that it would lead, to the Little Big Horn River. Here he found a village of almost unexampled extent, and at once attacked it with that portion of his force which was immediately at hand. Major Reno, with three companies. A, G, and M, of the regiment, was sent into the valley of the stream, at the point where the trail struck it. General Custer, with five companies, C, E, F, I, and L, attempted to enter it about 3 miles lower down. Reno forded the river, charged down its left bank, dismounted, and fought on foot until finally, completely overwhelmed by numbers, he was compelled to mount, recross the river, and seek a refuge on the high bluffs which overlook its right bank. Just as he recrossed, Captain Benteen, who, with three companies, D, H, and K, was some two miles to the left of Reno when the action commenced, but who had been ordered by General Custer to return, came to the river, and, rightly concluding that it was useless for his force to attempt to renew the fight in the valley, he joined Reno on the bluffs. Captain McDougall, with his company, B, was at first at some distance in the rear, with the train of pack-mules; he also came up to Reno. Soon this united force was nearly surrounded by Indians, many of whom, armed with rifles of long range, occupied positions which commanded the ground held by the cavalry — ground from which there was no escape. Rifle-pits were dug, and the fight was maintained, though with heavy loss, from about half past two o'clock of the 25th till 6 o'clock of the 26th, when the Indians withdrew from the valley, taking with them their village. Of the movements of General Custer and the five companies under his immediate command scarcely anything is known from those who witnessed them, for no officer or soldier who accompanied him has yet been found alive. His trail, from the point where Reno crossed the stream, passes along and in the rear of the crest of the bluffs on the right bank for nearly or quite three miles. Then it comes down the bank of the river, but at once diverges from it as if he had unsuccessfully attempted to cross; then turns upon itself, almost completes a circle, and ceases. It is marked by the remains of his officers and men and the bodies of his horses, some of them dotted along the path, others heaped in ravines and upon knolls, where halts appear to have been made. There is abundant evidence that a gallant resistance was offered by the troops, but that they were beset on all sides by overpowering numbers. The officers known to be killed are: General Custer, Captains Keogh, Yates, and Custer, Lieutenants Cook, Smith, McIntosh, Calhoun, Porter, Hodgson, Sturgis, and Riley, of the cavalry; Lieutenant Crittenden, of the Twentieth Infantry; and Acting Assistant Surgeon De Wolf, Lieutenant Harrington, of the cavalry, and Assistant Surgeon Lord are missing; Captain Benteen and Lieutenant Varnum, of the cavalry, are slightly wounded. Mr. Boston Custer, a brother, and Mr. Reed, a nephew, of General Custer, were with him and were killed. No other officers than those whom I have named are among the killed, wounded, and missing.

It is impossible as yet to obtain a nominal list of the enlisted men who were killed and wounded; but the number of killed, including officers, must reach 250; the number of wounded is 51. At the mouth of the Rosebud, I informed General Custer that I should take the supply-steamer *Far West* up the Yellowstone to ferry General Gibbon's column over the river; that I should personally accompany that column; and that it would, in all probability, reach the mouth of the Little Big Horn on the 26th instant. The steamer reached General Gibbon's troops, near the mouth of the Big Horn, early in the morning of the 24th, and at 4 o'clock in the afternoon all his men and animals were across the Yellowstone. At 5 o'clock, the column, consisting of five companies of the Seventh Infantry, four companies of the Second Cavalry, and a battery of three Gatling guns, marched out to and across Tullock's Creek. Starting soon after 5 o'clock in the morning of the 25th, the infantry made a march of twenty-two miles over the most difficult country which I have ever seen. In order that scouts might be sent into the valley of the Little Big Horn, the cavalry, with the battery, was then pushed on thirteen or fourteen miles farther, reaching camp at midnight. The scouts were sent out at half past 4 in the morning of the 26th. They soon discovered three Indians, who were at first supposed to be Sioux; but, when overtaken they proved to be Crows, who had been with General Custer. They brought the first intelligence of the battle. Their story was not credited. It was supposed that some fighting, perhaps severe fighting, had taken place; but it was not believed that disaster could have overtaken so large a force as twelve companies of cavalry. The infantry, which had broken camp very early, soon came up, and the whole column entered and moved up the valley of the Little Big Horn. During the afternoon efforts were made to send scouts through to what was supposed to be General Custer's position, to obtain information of the condition of affairs; but those who were sent out were driven back by parties of Indians, who, in increasing numbers, were seen hovering in General Gibbon's front. At twenty minutes before 9 o'clock in the evening, the infantry had marched between twenty-nine and thirty miles. The men were very weary and daylight was fading. The column was therefore halted for the night, at a point about eleven miles in a straight line above the mouth of the stream. This morning the movement was resumed, and, after a march of nine miles, Major Reno's intrenched position was reached. The withdrawal of the Indians from around Reno's command and from the valley was undoubtedly caused by the approach of General Gibbon's troops. Major Reno and Captain Benteen, both of whom are officers of great experience, accustomed to see large masses of mounted men, estimate the number of Indians engaged at not less than twenty-five hundred. Other officers think that the number was greater than this. The village in the valley was about three miles in length and about a mile in width. Besides the lodges proper, a great number of temporary brush-wood shelters was found in it, indicating that many men besides its proper inhabitants had gathered together there. Major Reno is very confident that there were a number of white men fighting with the Indians. It is believed that the loss of the Indians was large. I have as yet received no official reports in regard to the battle; but what is stated herein is gathered from the officers who were on the ground then and from those who have been over it since.

ALFRED H. TERRY,
Brigadier-General.

[Telegram]
Headquarters Department of Dakota.
Camp on Little Horn, June 28, 1876.
Assistant Adjutant-General,
Military Division of the Missouri, Chicago, Ill.:

The wounded were brought down from the bluffs last night and made as comfortable as our means would permit. To-day horse and hand litters have been constructed, and this evening we shall commence moving the wounded toward the mouth of the Little Big Horn, to which point I hope that the steamer has been able to come. The removal will occupy three or four days, as the marches must be short. A reconnaissance was made to-day by Captain Ball, of the Second Cavalry, along the trail made by the Indians when they left the valley. He reports that they divided into two parties, one of which kept the valley of Long Fork, making, he thinks, for the Big Horn Mountains; the other turned more to the eastward. He also discovered a very heavy trail leading into the valley that is not more than five days old. This trail is entirely distinct from the one which Custer followed, and would seem to show that at least two large bands united here just before the battle. The dead were all buried to-day.

ALFRED H. TERRY,
Brigadier-General.

[Telegram]
Headquarters Department of Dakota, Camp on Yellowstone, near Big Horn River, Montana,
July 2, 1876. Lieut. Gen. P. H. Sheridan, Chicago, Ill.:

In the evening of the 28th we commenced moving down the wounded, but were able to get on but four miles, as our hand-litters did not answer the purpose. The mule-litters did exceedingly well, but they were insufficient in number. The 20th, therefore, was spent in making a full supply of them. In the evening of the 20th we started again, and at 2 a m. of the 30th the wounded were placed on a steamer at the mouth of the Little Big Horn. The afternoon of the 30th, they were brought to the depot on the Yellowstone. I now send them by steamer to Fort Lincoln, and with them one of my aids, Capt. E. W. Smith, who will be able to answer any questions which you may desire to ask. I have brought down the troops to this point. They arrived to-night. They need refitting, particularly in the matter of transportation, before starting again. Although I had on the steamer a good supply of subsistence and forage, there are other things which we need, and I should hesitate to trust the boat again in the Big Horn.

Colonel Sheridan's dispatch informing me of the reported gathering of Indians on the Rosebud, reached me after I came down here. I hear nothing of General Crook's movements.

At least a hundred horses are needed to mount the cavalrymen now here.

ALFRED H. TERRY,
Brigadier-General.

For further details of the movements of Colonel Gibbon's column from the 21st to the 30th of June, I refer to his report.

For further details of the march of the Seventh Cavalry from the Rosebud to the Little Big Horn, and of the action of the 25th and 26th of June, I refer to the appended report of Major Reno, Seventh Cavalry.

When Colonel Gibbon's column left the Yellowstone the supply steamer *Far West*, upon which was Company B of the Sixth Infantry, was directed to make the attempt to ascend the Big Horn as far as the mouth of the Little Horn, in order that supplies might be near at hand to replace the scanty amount of subsistence which Colonel Gibbon's pack-animals were able to carry. Thanks to the zeal and energy displayed by Capt. Grant Marsh, the master of the steamer, the mouth of the Little Horn was reached by her, and she was of inestimable service in bringing down our wounded. They were sent upon her to Fort Lincoln.

The whole command reached the Yellowstone and went into camp on the north bank of the river on the 2d of July. Immediately afterward attempts were made to communicate with General Crook, in order that concert of action might be established between his forces and my own. The first and second of these efforts failed, the third succeeded. Three private soldiers of the Seventh Infantry, whose names, James Bell, William Evans, and Benjamin H. Stewart, deserve honorable mention here, succeeded in carrying a dispatch from me to General Crook, and two of them brought me his reply, from which I learned his own position and the position of the Indians. On the 15th of July, I received a telegraphic dispatch from the Lieutenant-General commanding, informing me that large re-enforcements would be sent to me. I had previously sent for recruits and horses for the Seventh Cavalry, and for guns to replace the Gatlings; and in order to increase my force, I determined to break up the depot on Powder River and bring the train and stores further up the Yellowstone.

Three possible lines for future operations presented themselves. The first by the left bank of the Big Horn; the second up Tullock's Creek; the third up the Rosebud, The second was inadmissible, for it was not practicable for wagons, and the pack-train which we had the means of improvising could not carry supplies for more than fifteen days. The first would have permitted wagons to be used, but it would have left between my own force and that of General Crook an almost, if not quite, impassable stream, the Big Horn, and besides would, if chosen, have rendered it necessary to keep a steamboat at the mouth of that river, while the Yellowstone was falling rapidly, and was already scarcely navigable to that point. The third line was therefore adopted. The depot was moved to the north bank of the Yellowstone, opposite the mouth of the Rosebud, and the troops from both above and below were brought to it.

The first of the re-enforcements sent to me, six companies of the Twenty-second Infantry, under Lieut. Col. E. S. Otis, arrived on the 1st of August.

On the 2d of August six companies of the Fifth Infantry, under Col. N. A. Miles [later General Nelson Miles], arrived. On the 2d the crossing of the river commenced. It was completed on the 7th, and on the 8th the march up the Rosebud began.

The column had been re-organized, and now consisted of a brigade of four battalions of infantry, under Colonel Gibbon.

The Seventh Cavalry, organized as eight companies, under Maj. J. A. Reno.

Four companies of the Second Cavalry, under Maj. J. S. Brisbin, and a battery of two ten-pound rifles and one twelve-pounder, under Lieut. W. H. Low, Twentieth Infantry, Major Brisbin was appointed chief of cavalry, on thestaff of the department commander, but still retained the immediate command of his battalion.

THE FIELD DIARY

of General A. H. Terry

A. Terry Brig. Genl.
4 BattalionsInf.
2 BattalionsCav.
1 BatteryArty.
Gift

[various mathematical calculations]

May 17th

Started from Ft. Lincoln Camp 5 A.M. Reached 1st Crossing of Little Heart River 2 P.M. With Main body Distance 13-1/2m.

May 18

Rev 3 A.M. Advance 5 A.M. Train across Heart River 8-1/2 A.M. Command moved 9 A.M. Halted 10.15 Reached Camp 2 P.M. Dist. 10.8m.

19th

Moved at 5. 3/4 of mile found ravine impassable from water. Turned back to camp & turned ravine. Marched 3/4 mile & halted for train to close up at 6 o'clk Halt to close up 7.20 (Morning threatening rain) very cloudy cleared at 6.30) (Hughes forward with Custer). Nooned 9 o'clk Halt 10 Start 10.35 Halt in camp 11.30 at 12 violent thunder storm with hail till 1-1/2. Great trouble getting train into camp. Some wagons not in till after six. Some required 10 & 12 mules to bring them in. Some left back on prairie Dis mcg detour 13-1/2m

20.

Started at 7.45 with advance guard arrived first crossing Creek at 9 o'clk dist. estimated 4-1/2m Started 11-1/2 halted Little Muddy 12 Bridge Started 2.45 Camp 3 March

21st

Reveille 3 Advance ordered at 5. Waited for construction of bridge over Little Muddy. Moved at 6.30. Marched till 7 Started again at 9. halted at 10. Moved again at 11. Halted at 12.10. With Advance guard. Moved 2.45 Arrived in camp 3.30 dist. 13-1/2

22d

Morning very bright & clear. Reveille 3. Advance 4.40 Halted at 3.40 on further edge of valley. Started 6.30 Halted 7.30 S 8.10 Halt 9.40 Camp 12 Dist. 15 1/3

23d

Bright & Clear Start 5.201 Halt 6.30 Start 7.05 H. 8.25

Camp on west plateau west of Young Men's Butte, great abundance of wood fine spring water good grass Dist. 7 3/4

24 Wednesday

Sunrise clear Rev. 3 Advance 4.55 Halt 6.40 Moved 7. Halt 8.10 Start Halt 9.50Reached camp 2 o'clk Dist. Near Stanley's Crossing 19.20

25 Thursday

Advance 4.45. Halted at hill beyond crossing till 6.30 Over valley country with easy slopes till 7.45 Advance over same country from 8.15 till 9.30 A. 10.5 Halt Build Bridge Moved 11.05 [?] Reached camp 2.20 Dist. 19.75m

26 Friday

Moved 5 A.M. Halt 5.30

Moved 6. Halt 7.10 Bridge Start 9.20

Halt 10.40 Moved 1 o'clk

27 Saturday

Rev. 3 Moved 5 Halt 6.15 Moved 8 o'clk Halt 9.20 This halt in sight of Meauvius Terres. Custer in advance with scouts & Wiers Co. seeking for trail. Sent Capt. Michaelis with 15 men & Pvt. McCue as guide to the South to find Stanley's Trail McCue comes to the conclusion that he had been mistaken, [rest too light on copy to be read]

Reynolds scouted to the South. Indians escort out Bearing of hills supposed to be the Sentinel Buttes shows us to be far South of Davis

Creek. Our course plotted on the map agrees with bearing. Turned back at 1 o'clk. Scout having reported that he had found Stanley's Trail to the northward Reached camp at 2.15 Encamped in valley of Creek. Dist. travelled 17 1/3m Probably a direct route would have been about 7 miles

28 Sunday

Advance 4.45 found advance guard 2 miles to the front. Reached 1st Crossing Davis Creek at 5.45 dist. 3.95m2 Crossing 1-1/2m

3 crossing— 200 yds. Time 6.45
3 crossing— 40 minutes
4 crossing— 2 hours
5 crossing— 1-1/4 hours
—
7 crossing— Reached 10-1/2

29th Monday

Left Camp 4.45 Arrived at Camp Main Column up left. Maguire to build bridge & pushed on to crossing reached it with advance guard at 6.20 Build bridge over crossing arrived at Little Missouri 8.30

30th

Remained in camp on Little Missouri. Sent Custer at 5 A.M. up the valley. Returned at 6 o'clk having made from 21 to 25 miles up & then same distance in returning No sign of Indians. Maguire at work building road at crossing of river. Went with Smith to reconnoiter road as far as the gable sided butte. Returned & sent Smith & Gibbs with 3 Cos to repair road. Rained heavily with lightning in evening.

31

Moved out of camp at 8 o'clk. Crossed river & moved with advance guard to crest near Gable Butte halted. Gibbs reported from rear that wagons pass river without trouble Wagons seen coming out of such without trouble. Reno comes up, Custer behind playing Wagon Master. Moved out with advance halted at 9.30 Odometer 5 1/3m The road through the bad lands, at this point is about four miles in length. Moved on at 11.30. Proceeded about two miles when a message was received from Lt. Col. Custer, *who left the column early in the day without any authority whatever* [emphasis added]. That we were not on Stanley's trail back [illegible] turned back &

examined ground [four words illegible] Moved on & reached camp at 2 o'clk Camp on one of the forks of Andrews Creek Dist. 10.9

June 1st Thursday

Commenced snowing at Midnight of Wednesday & at 1/2 past six A.M. of Thursday nearly or quite three inches of snow had fallen Snow continued to fall almost without interruption till late at night but during the day it melted more rapidly than it fell Remained in camp during day The snow being thick enough to obliterate the trail to make the feet of the animals "ball" badly and to make the track heavy

Had we gone on we should have made but ten miles for after having [illegible] that distance in advance no other is [illigible] fifteen or twenty miles. It did not seem to me worth while to put the command in motion in such weather & [illegible] them on snow for the sake of so short an advance of ten miles. Resumed in notes of May 31st that bad lands are limited to a strip of 4 miles on the river is erroneous. The most difficult part of this is of that width but they extend beyond the camp where we now are.

June 2d Friday

Snowed during night & slightly this morning Wind still in the same [illegible] N.W. Mud high. At noon snow ceased but still cloudy. Snow on ground rapidly disappearing ground wet but drying

Sent out Reynolds & Chf Wagon Master to examine road. Dr Williams thinking that to move to-day would be likely to bring on sickness, diarrhea & colds inasmuch as the weather lately has been so very bad A new camp would [illegible] Met Brown Wagon Master & Reynolds the guide sent out to examine road Reported good for two miles & a half then bad for a short distance and then good over rolling prairie. Ordered train to cross stream which runs through camp so as to be ready for start in the morning & sent out Maguire to look at bad part of road

June 3d

Started 5.45 Halt 6.55 Moved on to a wooded ravine & built a fire. Arrived at ravine at 8 o'clk Started 9 o'clk met scouts from stockade at 10.05 with despatches Halted 10 minutes & moved on. Halt 11.15 Advance 10 minutes past one Halt 2.55 Advanced 3.20 Reached Beaver Creek 4.25 Camped on East Bank Found Stanleys bridge partly carried away No wood to repair.

June 4

Advanced 4.55 Halt 6.15 Advanced 6.30 Halt 6.50 to build bridge on ravine

7.15 Halt at ravine to cut down bank 8.30 Start out at 9.40 Halt at crossing of Beaver Creek 12 N. Sent Reynolds & three men to explore to the front for water. Built bridge Commenced crossing at 2.15 Reached camp 2.35 Reynolds met on way to camping ground Left bank of Beaver reports no water within five miles Indian sign discovered here Three "Wickey-ups" with leaves still green Dist. 18 miles

June 5 Monday

Advanced 5 o'clk Marched 1.88m arrived at ravine or creek requiring a bridge Halted a short time. Then moved on over very fine rolling country with luxuriant grass. Halted at 7 o'clk Very heavy dew this morning. Notice heavy dew lately. Advanced 7.40 o'clk Halt on edge of bad lands 8.40 Dist 10.48m. Advanced 9.20 Halted at 10 o'clk to repair road. Moved on 10.30 Halt at Creek (Main Column) 12.15 Dist 18m Moved on 1.45 Reached camp by water in pools 2.20 Dis 20.5m

June 6 Tuesday

Advance 4.35 1st Halt 6.40A. 6.55 Halt O'Fallons 7.00(S. Fork) A.

8.45 Halt 10.10 Dist. 16m A. 11.05 Reached valley of O'Fallons 12 Halted to water in branch of O'Fallons 12.20 Discovered at this point that the guides had led us astray & that we were on the So. Fork O'F instead of the main stream retraced our steps & moved down the stream about 3 miles built a bridge crossed & went into camp.

7 Wednesday

Advanced 4.50 Halt 6.45 A. 7.10 H. 8.10 A 8.25 H 8.55 Bridge A 9.25 Halt on wooded ridge 10.35 A 11.35 Halt to excavate road 12.45 A. 1.30 Halt 2.50 Ravine Advance. —Halt cut road —Advance —Halt cut road

Advance 4.40 Advanced at edge of bluff Sent escort & line down thence back to find road for wagons. Repaired road Arrived at camp 6.55 Train arrived 9 o'clk Camp on branch of Powder River. Sent Scouts to mouth of river 10 P.M.

June 8th Thusday

Started from camp at 12 A.M. with Keoghs & Moylan's Companies 7th Cav. for mouth of the Powder. Marched till 2 o'clk halting 10 minutes Forded to right bank of river at 2.35 at head of island 1st Ford shallow, bottom hard [illegible] rather deep for wagons bottom hard stream very swift & evidently falling total width 1000 ft Reached 2d ford 3.25 Lost 1/2 hour hunting for wagon road to right found none If wagons do not take flat & [illegible] must go within land find river river bed 500 ft part not covered by water very soft under water find stoney banks steep much work for wagons to get up Water about horses belly

Marched on left bank through extremely rough country to point five miles from the mouth. After a long delay of nearly an hour found a ford impracticable for wagons Crossed Reached Steamer at 8 o'clk

9 Friday

Steamer started up river at 4 A.M. Met General Gibbon some distance below his camp at 11 o'clk Reached his camp at 12:30

Started to return at 1 o'clk Arrived at mouth of Powder 2.50 Started for camp 3.40 Heavy rain commenced at 4.10 & continued during March Found that river had risen & that the fords were considerably more difficult than the day before. Reached camp 9.50 Rain continued during night.

10th Saturday

Rained till 11 o'clk but not heavy. Issued orders for Reno to make a scout up the Powder to go to the forks of the Powder thence to go to the head of Mizpah Creek thence down to the mouth of Mizpah & then by Pumpkin Creek to Tongue River. Reno moved at 5 P.M. Sent men with his command to reconnoiter route on plateau on right bank of Powder to mouth Also Gibson to find pass to plateau Gibson did nothing.

11 Sunday

Men not returned, determined I must go instead. Custer with one Company the advance Self with Main Body. Started 5.50 Halt to make road 6.15 Successive halts for road making until 8 o'clk reached plateau marched on plateau -1/2 mile & halted Advanced at 9.30 at 10.30 halted at head of ravine to determine whether to follow Custer's trail or to cross the ravine perpendicularly [?] Wagons started on Custer's trail without authority therefore directed Column to follow Trail led to bottom lands of Powder Reached creek dry down banks bridged bottom & crossed by

Ascended again to plateau very high halted 12.20 Advanced at 12.55 Reached creek at 1.55 Halt to make road Moved on at 2.45 to plateau & halted at 1 main advance. Moved again at 4.05 Reached camp on Yellowstone 6.15.

12 Monday

[Steamer] *Far West* unloaded & despatched down the river at 12.30 to bring stores from stockade Mail sent by her.

13 Tuesday

Far West returned at —o'clk with stores.

14 Wednesday

Issued orders for Custer with 6 Cos 7th Cavalry & battery to start for Tongue River at 6 o'clk to-morrow morning. *Far West* to be loaded with 70 tons forage & 50 tons subsistence. 25 additional mules to be taken by Custer to replace any that may have become broken down in Reno's march. Band of 7th to remain at depot.

15th Thursday

Custer started at 7 o'clk Boat started Self & staff Baker's Co 6 Infty on Board.

At 5.30 15 miles from Powder River machinery broke down

16 Friday

Machinery repaired Started at 2.30 A.M. Buffalo rapids 7 h 8.20 o'clk [illegible] found water 6 ft Our spot only where a second attempt to get up necessary Arrived at Custer's camp 12.15

17 Saturday

At 8 A.M. on steamer to mouth of Tongue River Up Tongue River to head of branch of mouth which discharges near camp. Aground but too deep for fording. Probably boat could proceed further with careful navigation. Dist. up Tongue 500 yds A good position for a post at the junction of the Tongue & Yellowstone. South side of the Yellowstone West bank of Tongue. Plenty of wood for building & for fuel extensively for the latter. Yellowstone at Mouth of Tongue 800 ft estimated by firing from several volleys.

18 Sunday

Moved up the river short distance to cut wood Then returned to landing.

19th Monday

Lay at Landing in afternoon received despatches from Major Reno informing me that he had been to Mouth of Rosebud Also note from Gibbon.

Sent Hughes to meet Reno. Hughes returned at — Reno gave him no reason for his *disobedience of Orders.*

[*Custer later expressed that he thought Reno had lost a chance at glory for not having pursued the Indians whose camp he found, orders or no orders.—Ed*]

20 Tuesday

Directed Custer to cross Tongue & march to Reno's Camp, then to receive supplies from boat & thence go on to Rosebud with whole regiment. Reloaded boat & started on to Reno's Camp at 9,15 Reached Reno's camp at 12.30 landed some stores & then moved up to upper portion of camp & landed stores. Took on board Gatlings Sailed up river at 3.45 Tied up 9 o'clk.

21 Wednesday

Boat started—Reached Gibbons Camp 8.30 o'clk Left Gibbons at Rosebud 11.45 Returned down the river two miles to the better point selected by Custer for his Camp. At about 4 o'clk put Low's battery across the river Gave him instructions to follow the trial of Gibbons Column & report to Ball.

Sent 13 of the mules injured in Reno's march [with] Low for Gibbons Column.

22 Thursday

Sent Custer his orders in the morning. Custer started at 12 or 12.10 noon. Sent six Indian Scouts—Rees—to Powder River Depot with mail & with orders to Major—Moore to sent up *Josephine* with supplies at about 3 o'clk Steamer started up river soon after—Ran till 8.15

Friday 23

Still running up river. Tied up at 8.40—Said to be about 15 miles by river from Big Horn

Saturday 24th

Started out at —Stopped at Ft Pease at 5 o'clk. Took in wood Reached camp at — Orders given by Gen. Gibbon for immediate advancement. Landed detachment of Indian Scouts on right bank at 10.35. They having instructed to scout Tullocks Creek. Return at once for Cavalry to a point where the prairie ceases on the left bank. Ceases a mile above camp. Found Infty at boat required to cross Cavalry, Infantry & Artillery. At 4.15 Major Brisbin reported that Guides Taylor & — had found a good crossing of Tullocks.

Immediately ordered troops advance. They moved out at about five.

Gen. Gibbon sick on boat unable to move. Started in person with staff, orderlies & H. Qrs pack train at 6 o'clk P.M. Arrived at camp about 7.30 having been delayed by repacking mules. At about 8.45 Indian Scouts returned bring intelligence that they had seen buffalo running about six miles up the valley. One of them wounded by an arrow. Afraid to go further. Determined to move up the valley at 5 A.M. to-morrow. Sent orders to *Far West* to enter Big Horn at noon to-morrow & make [illegible] to mouth of Little Big Horn by noon the day after to-morrow past one.

25 Sunday

[*Unknown to Terry and Gibbon, this was the day Custer advanced on the Indians in the Valley of the Little Bighorn and died.—Ed.*]

Dr. Williams who was left with Gen. G. arrived in camp 4.45. Started 5.30 1st —Halt 6.35 A. 6.55 Turned to the right to gain the summit of the dividing ridge between Tullocks & Big Horn. Gained summit & halted at 7.55. Advanced 8.35. Halt 9.40 S 10 H 10.5 for battery which had broken pole S 11.20 H 12.20 Sent Mr. [Lieutenant James] Bradley* to left to scout ridge to look over to Little Horn. Started 12.45 and reached Big Horn at about half past one. Cavalry at about two o'clk sent up Big Horn 1-1/2 to 2 miles & unsaddled. Infantry & battery arrived about 3 o'clk Went forward to Cavalry about 4. Leave orders for Cavy to move about 5 o'clk for infantry to start next morning at least as early as 4 o'clk Started with cavalry & battery at 5-1/2 o'clk Commenced to rain rather heavily at times. Difficulties of the road at time almost indescribable especially in the dark. Captain Ball at first the guide. Finally one of the Crow Scouts undertook to reach a creek near Little Horn with grass & water. Found Creek & got into Camp about 12 o'clk. Battery obliged to [illegible] guns behind about ¼ mile from camp.

Bradley was scouting to the left of the Terry column on the 27th and he was the first to come across the dead on Custer's battlefield. James Bradley was killed at the Battle of Big Hole on August 9, 1877.

Ordered Scouts to be sent forward at daylight to find Ind. camp & guides to be sent back for Infantry. No fires or lights.

26th Monday

At ½ past seven Gen. B. brought note from Bradley Comdg Scouts saying that he had discovered fresh Indian trail. 4 Sioux who were not far from this camp. Taylor guide who had been sent to find route also reported two others. Had intended to await arrival of infantry but directed command to be ready to move as soon as men could get down coffee. Battery got in at 7.50. Started at 10 o'clk. Crossed small creek and moved on line beyond creek & halted for Infantry. Move on to a point 9-1/2 miles. Crossed Little Big Horn & halted to rest Infantry who had marched 22-1/2 miles. Advanced crossed creek 2.20. Marched out at 5.20. Halted 6.20. Before leaving creek sent two Scouts to communicate with Custer offering each $200 if they would get through. Scouts were Taylor and Bostwick. At about 6.40

Bostwick arrived back & reported Indians. Indians in parties of [illegible] or less [illegible] March continued until 8.40. Camp.

Tuesday, June 27th

Started at 7-1/2. 1-1/2 to 2 m out stopped 10 minutes. Then moved on to hill & at 8.20 saw a few tepes about 2 miles in front in bottom. Reached Reno's position about 11 o'clk. Troops encamped in bottom some distance below Reno's bluff. Wounded brought down to camp in bottom. Removal completed shortly after night fall. Supplies brought down. Sent messenger to find Steamer with orders in evening.

Wednesday June 28

Reno abandoned hill in morning. Moved down ridge & buried officers & men of Custer's five companies. Then came into valley & encamped on the right of Gibbon Moved camp about four miles down valley at 8.00 P.M. Great trouble with hand litters. Horse litters reported as doing well.

Thursday 29th

Ordered Lt. McGuire with one company of cavalry as escort to make survey of battlefield. Ordered poles to be prepared to make full compliment of horse litters. Litters completed & fording commenced & march commenced at 6½ P.M. Reached boat about 2 A.M. of the 30th Litters a great success.

Friday 30th

With wounded & lows guns started down river on steamer at 1.40. Arrived at Kirtlands camp at—.

Saturday July 1st

On boat at Kirtlands camp. Buried one of the wounded to-day. Stores unloaded.

Sunday July 2d

Removed wounded from boat in order to make room for troops to be ferried over. The Column arrived in the evening & were ferried across by ten o'clk.

Monday, July 3d

Sent Steamer *Far West* to Lincoln with wounded. Col. Smith sent on steamer with despatches & with orders to bring up some horses & supplies. Steamer started at about 12 o'clk

Thursday July 4th

Rode around picket line in morning & gave directions to establish two new posts.

Wednesday July 5th

Sent two detachments of Ree Scouts five men each to watch mouths of Rosebud &, Tongue [rivers]. Ordered General Gibbon to one company of Cavalry to scout as far as could be done in an advance of five days.

The company is to go to-morrow.

July 6th Thursday

Steamer *Josephine* arrived at 9 o'clk A.M. with stores. Captain Ball left camp at this morning for scout up the Yellowstone. Lt. Nowland reports only about 50 mules fit for service in 7th Cavalry —were killed & that the rest should be sent to Powder River

Friday July 7th

A party of seven Crows came into camp to-day searching for information of friends who were in the action. Report that General Crooks forces had a fight with Sioux about the 17th of June on Little Tongue River.* Sioux at first successful afterward driven back. I think that only Crooks advance guard engaged Main body in fight. Reported that Crook fell back to his wagon train after his fight One days march. Crook identified as commanding by shoulder straps and by beard.

General Crook fought the forces of Crazy Horse on June 17th on Rosebud Creek, not the Tongue River. Crook was required to withdraw for replacements and supplies and did not communicate with Terry and Custer before the Custer fight on the Little Bighorn.

Saturday July 8

The scouts C R Thomas[?] sent with despatches to general Crook. Returned having left gun & field glass. Says lost them on a raft crossing the Little Big Horn & was driven back by Indians. I don't believe his story. His horse came back the night before last.

Sunday July 9th

Received mail from Powder River bringing Genl Sheridan's despatches containing Genl Crooks account of his fight. Sent couriers with despatches to Genl Crook. Sent G. Herendeen to Crows with despatches for Gen Crook

Monday July 10

Capt Ball 2 Cav returned from scout to Pompey's Pillar. Had seen nothing.

Tuesday July 11

7 Cavalry moved camp about -1/2 mile down river in afternoon.

Tuesday July 12

Rode down to select camp for Gibbon below Reno. Found that no landing could be had without going below Ft. Pease ——[illegible]

Thursday July 13th No events

Friday July 14

Geo. Herendeen returned 8.15 from Crow camp. He had been unable to get Indians to carry despatches to Crook. Bro't news that from sixty to 100 Crows had come down or were on their way down to join us. A part of whom were already at mouth of Big Horn waiting for steamboat. Sent orders for Steamer to go in the morning & for Sangers Company to go as guard. Herendeen brought no news from Crook or from Ellis Saturday July 15th

Shortly after midnight of the 14th a furious thunderstorm set in, which flooded the camp. Water 4 to 5 inches deep in my tent. Crows crossed on boat 46 of them At 5 o'clk a violent hail storm with thunder. Received General Sheridan's despatches of the 7th vice Ft. Ellis at nightfall. Ordered the *Josephine* to be unloaded.

Sunday July 16th

Started on the *Josephine* down the river to meet the *Far West* 12.30 Moylan Co of 7th Cav & Sangers Co 17th Infty on board Gibbs, Hughes, & Nowland with me.

Monday July 17th

Arrived at Powder River 11.30 Commenced ferry our train in afternoon. *Far West* arrived from Bismarck after sundown.

Tuesday July 18th

Far West & *Josephine* both engaged in ferrying train during morning. Sent the Josephine to Bismarck Hughes on board with despatches & orders for rations

Wednesday July 19

Far West still engaged in ferrying

Thursday July 20

Far West still ferrying Completed ferrying Started up river at 3-1/2 o'clk P.M.

Friday July 21st

On *Far West* going up river In afternoon great difficulty in passing Buffalo Rapids. Obliged to cordelle.* Failed to get up Buffalo Stopped below for night.

*Use a towline especially as used on keelboats.

Saturday July 22d

Passed Buffalo by cordelle in morning. All rest of day good water.

Sunday 23

Good water to-day tho strong current & slow progress Left camp below mouth of Rosebud at 3 o'clk. Ran until about nine o'clk then found river too shallow laid up for night

Monday July 24

Wooded early Careful sounding from yawl showed less than three feet of water. Therefore fell back a mile & put off forage on left bank. Started on at 9.45 Almost immediately met scouts who report that Capt Wheelan 2 Cavalry with two Companies were close by. Waited till 10.45 for Wheelan. Directed him to return. Pretty good water till about 5-1/2 o'clk then great trouble at the shute which gave the most trouble [illegible] trip up. Passed the bad turn at about 9 o'clk.

Tuesday July 25th

Started at daylight. Boat seemed to make better speed than usual but lost much time getting in wood.

Wednesday July 26th

Reached camp at ——A.M.

Found despatches from Genl Crook. Gave orders for march of column to Rosebud. Loaded *Far West* with stores which train could not carry.

Thursday July 27th

Started on *Far West* for Rosebud at 10 A.M. Troops were to start at 11 o'clk Arrived at camp of Major Moore ordered to remove down to Rosebud.

Friday July 28th

Arrived at Rosebud at 6 A.M. Commenced unloading steamer at 7 Major Moore with his command & the train arrived & went into camp.

Saturday 29th

The steamer *Far West* having unloaded went up to the point above where the oats were landed & brought them down. Shortly before sundown *Far West* sent down to discover whether a report that a steamer was approaching was true Report false.

Sunday July 30th

Column from Big Horn Arrived about noon Gave orders for work of outfitting to commence as actively to-morrow. Ordered *Far West* to start to-morrow for Powder River for grain there and to go help other boats if in trouble.

Monday July 31st

Far West left for Powder River at day break this morning.

Tuesday Aug 1st

Steamer *Far West* arrived back at 9 A.M. with General Forsyth, Mil. Secy. Steamer Carroll arrived with Col Otis & 6 Cos 22 Inf & supplies. *Far West* left again for Powder River at noon.

Wednesday Aug 2

At 1 o'clk Carroll left with Gen. Forsyth for Bismarck. At 2 o'clk steamer Durfee arrived with Genl Miles six companies of 5th Inf & 150 cavalry recruits. At same time *Josephine* arrived back with supplies & guns & 64 horses.

Thursday Aug 3d

Josephine & *Durfee* employed in ferrying 2 Cavalry 7 Infanty & the Montana Train Friday Aug 4th

Josephine & *Durfee* employed in ferrying over train

Far West arrived back from Powder River with oats in bulk estimated at 150,000 pounds

Saturday 5th

Companies of 22d Infantry ferried over at 7 o'clk A.M. Ordered Companies of 5th Infty ferried over in afternoon.

Sunday 6th Aug

7 Cavy sent across river in morning then Moores battn 6th Inf then battery then Indian scouts. Teamsters moved over at 1 o'clk

Chf Q. M. reports one more day necessary to put train in order announced march to begin on 8th

Monday 7th Aug

Issued orders of organization & memoradum of order of march. Ordered revielle at 3 A.M. To march at 5 *Josephine* to go down river with surplus company property *Far West* to remain.

Tuesday Aug 8th

Started up Rosebud at 5 A.M. 2 Cav advance With Advance Day very hot Built bridges & crossings Marched 9-1/4 miles Went into camp at 2 o'clk to give time to build two different bridges.

Wednesday Aug 9th

Marched at 5 o'clk Road extremely difficult marched till 5 P.M. 11 miles. At about 2 P.M. some of the Crows returned bringing news that Sioux had been seen in front but saying that the six who had my despatches to Genl Crook would go through. At 31/2 Bravo was brought to me my despatch & informed that the six had fallen on with a large party of Sioux about 12 miles in front coming from the Tongue to the Rosebud Talked with Crows in evening. No definite estimation of number of Sioux Should think two or three hundred Perhaps the party which had been at the Powder River. Tried to get the Crows to make another attempt. Promised to have counsel.

Thursday Aug 10th

At 4-1/2 A.M. [Tom] Leforge reports that Crows after counsel refused to take despatches again, learned that 30 of them would push on this morning & endeavor to find out how many Sioux there are. Started at 5 o'clk Marched about 9 miles when Crows scouts came in & reported that large bodies of Sioux were coming down the valley (1.45 o'clk) Mounted men seen approaching & heavy dust seen apparently 2 to 3 miles in front Seventh Cavalry deployed as skimmishers 2 Cav in support. Commenced to park train. Buffalo Bill arrived & informed me that the men in front were Genl Crooks column Rode to the front met Genl Crook about 5 miles off. Column came up & went into camp Genl Crook left. Agreed with Gen Crook to follow Indians to-morrow.

Aug 11th Friday

Aug 10 Continued

Sent Miles with 4 Cos of his regiment to mouth of river then to take steamboat & proceed down river then to protect crossing

Tongue & Powder Sent 2 3 inch guns with him The remaining companies of regiment & 12 pdr gun to go down with train Ordered pack train to be fitted.

Aug 11th Friday

Morning occupied fitting team. Ordered wagons back Started at 11 o'clk Genl Crook's Column leading. Crossed ridge between Rosebud & Tongue reached camp 1/2 past 5. about 2 miles below crossing of Tongue & on right bank. Dist. 11 miles.

Aug 12 Saturday

Scouts sent out in morning to examine trail which appeared to be dividing Waited for them to return. Started 12-1/2 o'clk down the Tongue marched 13 miles went into camp Rain all day & following night very wet camp Dakota Column leading.

Sunday Aug. 13th

Infantry marched at 7 Cavalry soon after marched down river 24 miles. Cavalry reached camp at 4 o'clk Infantry at 7 o'clk Trail at times very strongly mark and at the last point of the march not more than 3 or 4 days old. The pony tracks having been made the day after the rain which we had on the Rosebud ie. on the 10th Letter to Miles at 9 o'clk

Monday Aug. 14

Infty marched at 6 o'clk Cavy at 7 Proceeded down Tongue to near mouth of Pumpkin Creek trail turned up Pumpkin Creek for — miles, then struck off to the North. Infantry of Gibbons Command very much tired from loss of sleep for two successive nights, went into camp on the Pumpkin. Distance marched 15-1/2 miles.

Tuesday Aug 15th

Marched at 6 o'clk crossed Ridge to Mizpah Creek & crossed it almost two miles above its junction with the Powder Crossed the Powder & went into camp Distance 20-1/2 miles.

Wednesday 16th

Marched at 6 o'clk down the Powder River passed one very large Indian Camp. Progress slow owing to bad crossing of river, ravines & gullies. Troops reached camp at wood opposite to camp of July 7th Troops arrived at 2 o'clk

Thursday Aug 17th

Started at 6 Took the ridge road Trail commenced to diverge & scatter about 18 miles from mouth of Powder. Rees started from camp at 6 o'clk to scout to Eastward. Reached camp at mouth of Powder at 2-1/2 o'clk Cavalry arrived soon after Infantry got in at 4.50 Distance 23 miles. Found that boat with Gen Miles left for Tongue River 16th in afternoon & had not returned. Need supplies aboard boat. Steamer returned about sunset Ordered steamer to go down to Glendive to ascertain whether Indians have crossed Miles on front.

Friday Aug 18th

In camp at mouth of Powder distributing rations Amount of subsistence up by 5000 rations than we ordered. Gen Miles having taken that amount for his men. About two days full forage. Saw Gen Crook in morning He proposed that I should wait & obtain more grain Stated that it would take two days for his animals to go back to point where trail turned off. Sent staff with message to Miles to turn back steamer. Moved camp of Infty & H. Qrs to site down river. Sent note to Crook saying that I tho't he ought not to wait rations, but he hope to give his animals more rest & grain. I would wait reply would see me in morning

Saturday Aug 19th

Consultation with Gen Crook in morning

Far West arrived at Rapids about 1/₂ past 4. Miles reports that no Indians have crossed the Yellowstone at Glendive Creek or this side of it. After consultation with Genl Crook & at his request sent *Far West* to Rosebud for forage shoes & subsistence.

Sunday Aug 20th

In camp Nothing new in morning In the evening Gen Miles brought mail & news told steamer *Carroll* was below with stores. Snakes Utes & Crows left for horses.

Monday Aug 21st

Steamer *Carroll* arrived up 5 o'clk Wagon Train reported in sight.

Tuesday Aug 22d

Wagon train arrived in good condition Officers of *Carroll* reported that it would be impossible to come above Wolf Rapids even if the cargo should be taken off boat.

Ordered thirty five set mule trains to be made up for movement to Little Missouri & *Carroll* to cross them below rapids.

Scout Taylor arrived in afternoon reported *Far West* aground at Buffalo Rapids & discharging cargo.

[various mathematical calculations and page torn in half]
[various mathematical calculations and page torn in half]
[various mathematical calculations and page torn in half]
[various mathematical calculations and page torn in half]
[blank]
[various mathematical calculations]
[various mathematical calculations Drawings of heads in profile Page torn in half]
[various mathematical calculations and page torn in half]
Lewis Practised Prowl [?] Boat An Egg Farm by H. K. Stoddard
[various mathematical calculations and page torn in half]

Washing 12 Hdk fo[?]
Shirts ///
Woolen undershirts / /
Towels / / / /
Wollen over shirts 2
Nightshirt /
Trousers ///
Musquito netting /
Stockings / / pair Eleven from

[all of the above was crossed out and page torn at this point]

76 [various mathematical calculations and two heads drawn in profile]

Infty—180

Infty—240

Infty—240

Lows Battery—26

Moore Comd—470

Battery of Art—60

7 Cavalry—275

1491

2d Cavalry—160

1651

[various mathematical calculations and head drawn in ¾ view]

Mouth of Powder River
[various mathematical calculations]

Insufficient in trouble more to be sent

[various mathematical calculations]

Living

Reno
Wier
Benteen
French
Moylan
McDougall
Godfrey
Edgerly
Hare
Wallace
Mathey – DeRudio
Varnum – Gibson
A.A. Surgeon Porter

Known to be killed

Hodgson
McIntosh
(AA Surgeon De Wolf)
Gen. Custer
Capt Keogh
Lt. Cook adj.
Capt Yates
Capt Custer
Lt A E Smith
Lieut Calhoun [crossed out; not sure why this is crossed out. Calhoun, Custer's brother-in-law, was killed on Calhoun Ridge.]
Lt J. E. Porter
Lt Harrington [crossed out]
Lt Sturgis
Lt Crittenden
Lt Reilly

Dr. Lord [crossed out]
Mr. [Boston] Custer [one of Custer's brothers]

Mr. [Autie] Reed [Custer's 17-year-old nephew]
Isaiah [Dorman, interpreter, the only African-American on the expedition]

Remaining men wounded & unwounded 329 wounded about 40

[various mathematical calculations

[various mathematical calculations]

[various mathematical calculations and two heads drawn in profile]

[various mathematical calculations and page torn in half]

Horses

Officers at Lincoln

Ammunition for cavalry [crossed out]

Gatling Guns

Pack saddles

Pack Mules

Recruits

Men 7 Cav at Powder River Clothing 7 Cav Ammunition for Gatlings Clothing for Infantry

Cos 7 Cav —152
H Tr—4
Custer —2
Medical —2
Reno —2

N.C.S. —1
Packers —1
Scouts one Officer 5
Guides & Int. —1
Battery in C Officers [page torn off here] 3

Pack Mules
Hay Board
Receipt to Michaelis
Telegraph
Water for Rice Paid
Rice knife

[various mathematical calculations]

[various mathematical calculations and head drawn in profile]

Pistol number 4507

[various mathematical calculations]
[various mathematical calculations]
[various mathematical calculations]
[various mathematical calculations and head drawn in profile]
[various mathematical calculations]
[various mathematical calculations]
[various mathematical calculations]
[various mathematical calculations]
[various mathematical calculations]
[various mathematical calculations]
Assignments of post/quarters of officers Guides
Interpreters
[?] of Expedtion
Com. Yellowstone
Rule
Orders
Medical Matters Thompson Commissary Nowlan Wa. Train Horses for Seward

END OF DIARY

Get your FREE EBOOK—join our mailing list to get notified of great new (old) books and the latest blog posts.

BIG BYTE BOOKS is your source for great lost history!

Made in the USA
Lexington, KY
24 October 2017